Irelaı

Travelers!

*The Tourist Guide To Make The Most
Out Of Your Trip To Ireland – Discover
Where To Go, Eat, Sleep & Party*

Copyright

Table of Contents

Introduction

I want to thank you and congratulate you for downloading the book, *"Ireland: For Travelers! The Tourist Guide To Make The Most Out Of Your Trip To Ireland – Discover Where To Go, Eat, Sleep & Party"*.

This book has all the information you need to make your visit to Ireland worthwhile and memorable.

What do you think of when you think of Ireland even with the fact that it isn't so popular in the news? Well, at first, I thought of it as a country of drunks; the Irish people love their drink! But what else do you think of? Do you know that Ireland has many great minds than you have ever thought of? Think of the father of chemistry, Robert Boyle and the Earls of Rose, which boasted of the world's largest telescope for years and a lot more. Well, Ireland is not just about the people and their traditions; it has a rich culture, beautiful scenery, breathtaking attractions, and a lot more things. This is just a MUST visit destination.

Thanks again for downloading this book, I hope you enjoy it!

When you are looking for a travel destination, you want to gain the most out of visiting the area. You want to travel to an area that is rich in culture, history, scenic locations, culinary experiences, and recreational activities. Ireland has all this plus more. Many who visit this captivating place end up coming back and for good reason. After all, there aren't many places that can boast of birthing pioneering investors, giants as far as technology is concerned, and still manage to preserve the authenticity that comes with a rich culture.

Among the things that capture people's hearts is that back in time experience they get when visiting Ireland. This land has fairytale castles, saints and a mastery of storytelling. Also this land is known as the ancestral land of many American presidents. Is it any wonder that many movies based on giants and dragons are set in Ireland? Well, that is just the tip of the iceberg of what this country has to offer. Follow through as we explore the many possibilities.

Country

Ireland is an island found in Western Europe. As a country, Ireland is divided into the Republic of Ireland and Northern Ireland. This is because Gaelic Ireland (that came into being in the first century) was conquered during the Norman invasion (twelfth century) and came under the rule of England. In 1801, Ireland joined other countries to form the United Kingdom. This did not last long however, as eventually, there was a rebellion and the Republic of

Ireland broke away to gain its sovereignty while Northern Ireland remained as part of the United Kingdom. Nowadays, the Republic of Ireland remains the largest, resting on five-sixths of the land while the Northern Ireland occupies the rest.

Regions of the country

The traditional Ireland boasted of thirty-two counties, although this number did not show the full picture as some of the counties did not run as normal counties. However, as far as tourism and travel is concerned, the country is divided into seven regions. These are:

The North West

The North West Region includes Sligo, Cavan, Monoghan, Donegal and Leitrim counties. It is known as one of the regions of romance. The English novelist, Trollope, had a stint as a Postmaster in Leitrim and he ended up inventing the post box.

The South West

The South West region is home to the scenic counties of Cork and Kerry. Here, you will find the incredible Rings of Kerry as well as Carrantuo hill, the highest point in Ireland. You can also explore the Blarney Castle and visit Blennerville and Cobh Harbor. Cobh Harbor made history by being the last port of call for the famous Titanic.

The South East

The South East region is made of Waterford, Kilkenny, South Tipperary, Carlow and Wexford counties. The oldest city in the South East region as well as the rest of Ireland is Waterford. The famous Waterford Crystal is stationed here. The South East region also has the bragging rights of hosting the ancestors of Diana (Princess of Wales). You can find the impressive portraits of butlers housed at the Long Gallery in Kilkenny. And for those who find joy in Opera, there is a whole Opera Festival that is carried out each year in Wexford.

The West

The West region is home to Mayo, Roscommon, and Galway counties. The West region also offers a candid look into various religions. It hosts both religious shrines and ancient pagan monuments. It is also home to Crough Patrick, the well known landmark that was blessed by St. Patrick. Every July, the Faithful embark on climbing this landmark.

The East Coast and Midlands

The East Coast and Midlands region includes the counties of Westmeath, Meath, Laois, Kildare, north Offaly, Wicklow, Loouth and Longford. The region has lush gardens, great castles and impressive cathedrals and beaches. It is also the site of the 'Druid Fire Cult' as well as the host of the Hill of Uisneach and the Samhain Festival. Many historians have traced Halloween to this very region.

Shannon Region

If you want a taste of the ancient times, Shannon region is the place to be. Shannon region includes the Clare Counties. The river Shannon provides water for the pastoral activities carried out by other counties such as Limerick and North Tipperary. It is in Liscannor, Co. Clare that the submarine was born. This is the place John Holland decided to invent the submarine after observing the effect of the Atlantic waves on water vessels (the vessels were submerged in water for most of the time).

Northern Ireland

This region is part of the United Kingdom. It includes the counties of Armagh, Fermanagh, Antrim, Down, Londonderry and Tyrone. Northern Ireland is known as home of the Giant's Causeway. It is also the land where many American presidents came from. However, apart from being the ancestral land of presidents, it is also the country of St. Patrick. In fact, his gravesite can be found at Downpatrick.

All these regions have numerous attractions and activities that you can enjoy. This, however, means that you have to know where to stay in order to make the most out of your trip.

Where To Stay

You can find different types of accommodation when you visit Ireland. Your accommodation will of course depend on how many people you are travelling with, the amount of cash you want to use, the experience, adventure you are looking for and your personal preference. You can find:

B&Bs

These family run accommodations offer bed and breakfast. If you want to get that local feeling and explore local sightings, this is the accommodation type you should seek. Irish B&Bs range from farmhouses, to cottages and city townhouses.

Guesthouses

A guesthouse is especially attractive if you are looking for some privacy without having to incur the cost of a hotel. They are run professionally and ensure that you have security, comfort, and relaxation.

Self-catering

Sometimes you just require somewhere to stay without needing the other services as offered by a hotel. If you are travelling with friends or family, a self-catering home will suit you well. You can choose to live in a cottage, a townhouse, or even a holiday home. You get the opportunity to do things for yourself and thus have more privacy.

Hostels

Hostels offer the opportunity to mix with an eclectic group of traveling individuals who have come to enjoy Ireland. You get your own bedroom and self-catering kitchen facilities. There are also lounge areas where you can go to relax in.

Hotels

Many Irish hotels are registered and graded by Failte Ireland. This means they have been inspected for quality and graded accordingly. Most hotels offer:

Caravan and Camping

If you are looking for adventure or you just want to camp, you can bring a tent or a caravan. Ireland has many parks so you will not be short of parks to camp in. You can find a family run park or a huge park that has more people in it. Many parks strive to include leisure activities on site. This means you will be well occupied.

Pubs (that have accommodation)

Some pubs have accommodation facilities and they offer bed and breakfast. If you want to enjoy the pub life without the inconvenience of having to travel for long distances to your hotel room, you should consider pubs.

Before you choose a place to stay, it is advisable that you do more research on it. This way, you will find out if the place is suitable for your traveling needs and if it can accommodate all your needs. Some of the places you can try include:

The North West Region

Name of hotel: Radisson Blu Farnham Estate Hotel

Location: Cavan

Charges per night: from €139

Website/phone number: www.radissonblu.ie / +353 49 437 7700

South East Region

Name of hotel: Seven Oaks Hotel

Location: Carlow

Charges per night: from €70

Website/phone number: www.sevenoakshotel.com / +353 59 913 1308

The West

Name of hotel: Pillo Hotel Galway

Location: Galway

Charges per night: from €109

Website/phone number: www.pillohotelgalway.com / +353 91 513 200

Shannon Region

Name of hotel: Park Inn

Location: Clare

Charges per night: from €71

Website/phone number: www.parkinn.ie / +353 61 471 122

The South West Region

Name of hotel: Killarney Royal

Location: Kerry

Charges per night: from € 113

Website/phone number: www.killarneyroyal.ie / +353 64 663 1853

Northern Ireland Hotels

Name of hotel: Chimney Corner Hotel

Location: Antrim

Charges per night: from €51

Website/phone number: www.chimneycorner.co.uk / +44 28 9084 4925

How To Get Around

Once you decide where you are going to stay and what you are going to see, the next step is to decide how to get there. There are many ways to travel in Ireland. These are:

Air

Despite your best intentions to explore Ireland, you may be constricted by time. You may not have the leisure to hike or cycle to your destination of choice. If this is the case, you can save some time by traveling by air especially if you are going to the outlying areas. You can take a scheduled flight from Dublin (if you are in the Republic) or from Belfast (if you are in Northern Ireland). Air fares range from €20 to €100. This depends on what season it is and the demand for air travel.

Bus

Traveling by bus is often wise especially if you have no idea where you are going. This is because buses come with bus schedules. You can easily view the routes you will take, the timetables and the fares. You can also get cheap deals when it comes to ticket prices. Check out www.buseireann.ie for your schedules and fare prices.

Car

You can rent a car in Ireland. However, you need to carry with you your original driving license (not a photocopy). If you are not from an EU country, you need to have an

International Driving Permit. Apart from your driving license, you also need to have the registration document and ensure that your insurance will cover driving in Ireland.

Bicycle

Traveling by bicycle is one of the best ways to enjoy the scenery in Ireland. Unfortunately, there are not many bike rentals available. This means you have to plan ahead to ensure that you book your bike in time. Eurotrek Raleigh (www.raleigh.ie) is the place to go when you need a bike as they have agents all over the country. You need to ensure your bike is in top form when you collect it to avoid unnecessary disasters. Check the brakes, the tires, the pump, and the repair kit to ensure that everything is working properly.

Rail

If you plan your travel well, you can benefit greatly from rail transport. Irish Rail (www.irishwail.ie) and Translink (www.translink.co.uk) are responsible for train services in the Republic and Northern Ireland respectively. Ensure that you check out the train routes and fares before setting out on your journey because some counties have few links between them and others don't even use train services.

It would be best to ensure that you always carry a map with you even if you have an idea as to where you are going. This way, you can see your route and anticipate the things you will see as you travel.

Top Experiences

Ireland is a land full of diversity and beauty. Some of the top experiences you can be a part of are:

Giant's Causeway

The story goes that once upon a time in County Antrim, Northern Ireland, there existed two rival giants – Finn, from Ireland and Benandonner from Scotland. Finn issued a challenge and proceeded to build a causeway of stones in the water, as Benandonner could not fit in a boat. However, once Benandonner accepted the challenge and came to Ireland, Finn fled in fear because the latter was bigger than he had imagined. Finn quickly fled to the hills and his wife cleverly disguised him as a baby. When Benandonner saw the 'baby' he trembled in fear because he thought surely the father would be much bigger. Benandonner ran back home ensuring that he ripped the causeway to prevent Finn from following him. That is the story of the formation of the Giant's Causeway. However, the coastal area that has about forty thousand basalt columns was formed due to a volcanic eruption that happened millions of years ago. It is simple a sight to behold.

Titanic Belfast

Who has not heard of the tragic story of the Titanic? Well, hearing about it and experiencing a part of what actually went down are two very different things. Now imagine a town dedicated to tell the story of the Titanic. Titanic Belfast is not just a drop in the ocean; it is a world-class exhibition that will take you from the heart of the ship to the Atlantic wreckage site. What's more, it will offer you clanking shipyard rides.

Gaelic Football Match

A Gaelic Football match is unlike any other match you have ever seen. You have to experience it for yourself to understand its true significance. Yes, the county rivals sweat it out on the fields but it is the spectators (and their commentary) that keep the volume on blast and offer differing points of view that go hand in hand with the local GAA matches.

Game of thrones, Castle ward

No doubt, one of the things that brought more attention to Northern Ireland is the Game of Thrones. The drama, the mystery, the deception, the alliances – there are few who wouldn't want to see the place where the intriguing show is filmed. But apart from becoming a curious observer, you can take up archery lessons in archery at the Castle Ward Estate (House Stark).

The Rock of Cashel

When you hear the word 'rock', you picture an unassuming rock that has somehow caught the attention of people. Well, there is nothing ordinary about the Rock of Cashel. It was a symbol of power. The Rock of Cashel is situated in County Tipperary's plains. You can find ancient religious structures that date back more than 1000 years. The Rock of Chapel was what designated who the seat of power belonged to. In this case, it determined the kings and churchmen who were rulers over the region.

The Cliffs of Moher

Over one million individuals make the trek to visit the cliffs of Moher each year and for good reason. This breathtaking place makes you forget that you are with company and leaves you contemplating the wonders of nature. The Cliffs themselves stretch for about five miles. They rise over seven hundred feet (702 feet) over the Atlantic Ocean waters. As such, they provide a stunning view into the surrounding and you will be able to see Islands, Bays and Mountains right from the Cliffs.

Boyne Valley

There is a reason why the Boyne Palace is a designated World Heritage Site. One of the features that continue to astound to this day is the massive megalithic ancient passage tombs. Modern man with all his wisdom has failed to explain how the tombs of Kwoth, Dowth and especially Newgrange came to be. And every year (on Dec 21) during the Winter solstice, a beam of sunlight shines forth through a roof box that was specially designed. It is simply breathtaking.

The Dingle Peninsula

Expect to meet Fungi in the Dingle Peninsula (no, not the fungus but the celebrity Dolphin that has melted hearts for years). Dingle is a serene place that you can just relax and enjoy your time in the water as you travel by boat. You can also have a pint and try putting the toasted Irish oats ice cream.

The Ring of Kerry

If there's only one place you can see in Ireland, check out the Ring of Kerry. This is the place fairytales are woven. It showcases Ireland as a spectacular, romantic place. Kerry possesses some of the most revered ancient monuments, stunning scenery, and romantic castles. You can view beehive huts, ruined monastery, the Neolithic stone circle, and Gardens. You can also enjoy beautiful writings and a mouth-watering cuisine.

Aran Islands

Ireland is truthfully the island made up of other islands. It has numerous islands each with its own uniqueness. One of the most popular islands is the Aran Islands. This is a region that consists of three islands (Inishinor, Inishmaan and Inisheer) that have refused to let go of their ancestral mystique. Aran Islands is so well preserved as far as culture goes that Celtic Spirit (founded by Elizabeth Zellinger) offers classes and workshops to those who want to learn about the people of Aran Islands.

Cultural Experiences

Culture describes the way of life of a people. When you understand what influences people and where they are coming from, you will be able to better appreciate where they are in the present. Ireland has a rich culture and many parts of it still hold onto that culture of those before them. You can learn more about the culture of the people from various cultural experiences. These are:

Trad

Few things sing of the culture of a people like traditional music. Music, drinking, and storytelling go hand in hand when you are in Ireland. The pubs come alive especially at night with 'Trad', that is, the traditional music that keeps people dancing and laughing. It is quite normal to hear music accompanied by tin whistles, accordions, and fiddles. As a matter of fact, Doolin, a small village in Clare County is recognized as the heart of Irish music but that doesn't stop the people from showcasing their music wherever they are.

Literary Dublin

It's not often that one area produces multiple Nobel Prize winners for a particular category. Well, Ireland has not one but four (and counting) Nobel Prize winners for Literature. In fact, the Dublin Writers Museum is dedicated to showcasing gems such as audio recordings, letters, manuscripts, and books.

Trinity College – Book of Kells

Let's face it, buildings that were built in the olden days trump many buildings built today. Trinity College stands tall as Ireland's most prestigious college and literary heritage (just don't let the University College Dublin hear you say that). Trinity College is simply magnificent. Queen Elizabeth founded it in 1592 and since then it continues to be a center of great architecture and excellence. Trinity college houses both the Book of Kells and the Long Room section of the old library that is said to be the inspiration for Jedi Archives (from Star Wars: Attack of the Clones).

Guinness Storehouse

It is said that few people would try to out drink like an Irishman. Ireland is known as the country with more pubs than hotels. It is here that the world known Guinness stems from. Guinness is one of the best known exports in Ireland and the story of its origin is well told in the Guinness Storehouse. Imagine walking through a building whose core is shaped as a giant pint glass. A guide takes you through the inspiring history of how Guinness came to dominate the market and once you reach the top floor of the building, you encounter the Gravity Bar and sip a complimentary pint of Guinness. You end up being inspired and satisfied.

Culinary Adventure

Once upon a time, visitors joked about the many ways to cook potatoes in Ireland – that was before the culinary revolution. Nowadays, you will be spoiled for choice as you explore Ireland's culinary scene. There are many venues you can experience a culinary adventure in. These are:

One Pico in Dublin

One Pico is an award-winning restaurant that serves a variety of dishes from starters to main courses to dessert and cheese. You can enjoy seared Mackerel, Pan-fried Hake, Quail, seared Scallops and Pineapple tart tatin among other foods.

Cliff House in Ardmore, County Westford

The Cliff House Hotel is one hotel that does not lack in appetizing food. It has a Michelin-starred restaurant that introduces you to a variety of spectacular dishes.

Wuff in Dublin

Wuff is the place to go during the weekends (or any other day). It is a Bistro that serves breakfast, brunch, lunch, and dinner although you will have to make alternative dinner plans on Thursday, Friday and Saturday nights. Visit www.wuff.ie for reservations.

Las Rada in Kildare

Las Rada Tapas and Wine Bar is well known for the tapas-style of dining. This allows guests to be introduced to and to explore new tastes. This way, you get to taste many mouth-watering dishes that you probably wouldn't have known to try out.

English Market in Cork city

Since 1788, the English Market has been serving Cork City and its environs. The market has a variety of products and its traders offer personalized service to the visitors. You can get organic products as well as new products unique to the region. The English Market should be part of your weekly visit especially if you stay in self-catering facilities.

The Temple Bar Food Market in Dublin

Temple Bar Food Market is open every Saturday from 10am up to 4.30pm. The market is hosted at Meeting House Square under a retractable canopy. You should definitely check out the market especially if you intend to make a stop at the Temple Bar.

So, what should you eat in such places?

Potatoes are a main ingredient in many of Ireland's dishes. Here are some of the dishes that you should probably order to get a taste of Ireland's culinary wealth.

*Coddle or simply Dublin Coddle: This dish looks like some sort of watery stew but with some pork sausages and rashers. It doesn't really look good but it is damn delicious.

*Blaa Blaa Blaa: This is a bread bun with some more flour on the outside. Some will even have pork sausages and rashers in there.

*Rashers: These are usually thin and fatty cuts of bacon

*Black and white pudding: You will love it.

*Drisheen: Well, this is simply pudding that is made using sheep's intestines that is usually filled with sheep's blood and meat.

*Baked Beans: You will love the Irish version. These are very common at many B&Bs and hotels in Ireland.

*Potato Farls

*Colcannon

*Boxty

Nature And Adventures

Of course, one of the major reasons visitors flock to Ireland each year is to experience the nature and partake in adventurous activities. Here are some of the top outdoor activities you can engage in during your visit to Ireland.

Cycling and walking

There's something about walking and cycling that takes you closer to nature. And it's even better when you don't have to encounter traffic while you do those two things. Well, forget Tour De France; the place to go is the Great Western Greenway. This 42km, world-class facility following the line of Westport right up to Achill Island Railway gives you the opportunity to explore nature; you don't have to be extra fit to attempt it. Here is a map to give you a glimpse of what you can expect to experience.

Water trails

The human body gravitates towards water (unless of course you are among the few who don't value water). Water trails have gained in popularity simply because individuals want to explore and have adventures in the water much like the ones they would have on land. The Blueway water trail for instance stretches from North West Mayo right up to South Galway. And as you explore it, you can snorkel or go kayaking.

Dolphin and whale watching

Dolphins and whales have always fascinated human beings. They are the closest things to the sea monsters that legends spoke of – the ones that existed before the ice age. There is a special area of conversation, The Shannon Estuary, where you can view the rare bottlenose dolphins. The best thing about these tours is that you can watch the dolphins or whales from the comfort of the boat.

Mayo horse drawn caravan holidays

When you are in Ireland, horse drawn caravans are not just a thing of the past. Caravan providers such as www.horsedrawncaravan.com will provide a caravan for you, teach you how to operate, and accompany you until you get your footing. The caravans come with self-catering facilities so you will be able to explore the land at your leisure.

Kayaking

The Ring of Kerry is a popular place to drive around while you are in Ireland. However, if you are more adventurous, try kayaking. This way, you will be able to have the inside view instead of just marveling at the sights in awe from a distance. You will learn how to ride the rapids and you will see interesting flora and fauna. Guides are always available to lead you through your adventure.

Canoe trail in County Down

Northern Ireland has embraced canoe trails in the recent years. This started with the successful 30-mile Lough Erne's trail and soon afterwards other trails started coming up. A canoe enables you to have the feeling of entering paradise. While you are in the canoe, you are part of the water and not just an outside observer.

Stay in a fishing village in Donegal

Imagine staying in your own self-catering place in a fishing village. Donegal offers such a place. It allows tourists to experience all the joys of the simple life. The story of Donegal is uplifting indeed. It started with the residents who found that fishing business was no longer thriving. Instead of giving up and leaving town, they restored their town and set it up as a tourist village allowing tourists to travel on fishing boats.

Seaweed foraging

Seaweed is well known in Ireland, not just as food but also as medicine and fertilizer. However, instead of just sitting down and ordering a meal, you can forage for seaweed in West Cork. This way, you will get the whole experience and have a tasty meal in the end.

Archery

Archery is not a sport you would normally undertake simply because there are rules against shooting arrows whenever you feel like (you could hurt someone). However, a visit to places such as Castle Ward will provide you with the opportunity to shoot all the arrows you like (without the fear of hitting the wrong target).

Climbing and Abseiling

Of course, we can't forget about climbing and abseiling when we talk about adventure and outdoor activities. Climbing challenges you to exert yourself and abseiling will challenge you to face your fears. Fortunately, there are many hills and cliffs to be climbed in Ireland.

Places To Recharge

Sometimes you go on vacation just to recharge after many months of living a fast-paced life. You want to experience the peace and tranquility while at the same time experience beautiful scenery and a life away from your normal routine. There are many places where you can recharge. These are:

The Lakelands

As the name suggests, the Lakelands is a stunning destination that showcases lakeshores. You can enjoy activities such as horse riding, cycling, walking, and many others. The Lakelands is divided into four route sections. These are Lough Ernell, Lough Derg, Lough Ree and Upper Lakelands.

The Wild Atlantic Way

Instead of setting for only one county, you can travel the Wild Atlantic Way. This coastal route will take you to seven counties and you will get to enjoy the breathtaking scenery. There are various things to discover at each point and you will not be disappointed as you go through Donegal, Galway, Kerry, Cork, Mayo, and Clare.

Cork's Islands

Ireland is a country that is definitely filled with many islands. When you want to recharge, you will get pleasure visiting the islands and embracing the island life. The Cork Islands offer such pleasure. You can visit the islands of

Bere Island, Cape Clear, Long Island, Heir Island, Sherkin Island and Whiddy Island. Here you will find gourmet food, scenic landscapes, rich culture and heritage as well as beautiful wildlife.

Vandeleur Walled Gardens

Discovering unusual plants as you take a nature walk is one way to recharge your body and mind. Vandeleur Walled Gardens are found in County Clare. They cover about 170 acres and though previously neglected, the gardens and woodlands are now kept in lush shape.

Castle Dargan

Not many hotels around the world can boast of sitting pretty surrounded by 170 acres of mature woodlands. In fact, very few can. Catsle Dargan, a hotel located in Sligo town is truly unique. As the name suggests, the cornerstone of the hotel is the Castle Dargan House. The Castle ruins are a story in themselves. The warm friendly service, log fires, scenic scenes, and quiet times will have you rejuvenated in no time.

Cherryville House

If you are tired of the fast-paced city life, go ahead and relax at Cherryville House in Kildare. This is a Bed and Breakfast that has cattle, chicken, ducks, cats, and even a dog. In other words, it is a traditional style farmhouse that allows you to enjoy a quiet rural setting.

Radisson Blu & Spa

If you are at Rosses Point, Sligo, the place to stay is Raddisson Blu & Spa. The hotel is situated in such a way that you can enjoy both business and leisure activities without feeling rushed. You can enjoy outdoor activities such as angling or golfing or you can get the full spa treatment and pampering. You can also explore what the vibrant County Sligo has to offer.

Other Major Attractions

Ireland is full of attractions. In fact, it would take you quite awhile to explore all there is to this beautiful Island. Some of the major attractions include:

Killarney National Park

Killarney National Park is a wonderful place indeed. This park has woodlands, mountains, and lakes. It contains rare insects, fish and birds, as well as native red deer. You can also catch a glimpse of the white-tailed sea eagle.

The Burren

People travel to Ireland just to see the Burren. This rocky mass made of limestone karst plates continues to facilitate botanists and geologists alike. This is because it has both alpine and Mediterranean plants – plants that are not usually found together in Ireland. The number of species is said to be 635 and counting – a botanical paradise indeed.

St. Patrick's Cathedral

Who can forget St. Patrick's Cathedral when they visit Dublin? This place has a lot of history and a lot of meaning. But despite its history, it has not been designated to museum status. People still go to services there each day. St. Patrick's is where the author of Gulliver's Travel,

Jonathan Swift, is buried. It is also the first place that Handel's 'Messiah' was performed.

Croke Park

Ireland is big on hurling and Gaelic football. In fact, these two are national sports and they are played at the Croke Park. The park has a capacity of eighty thousand and it symbolizes the Irish cultural nationalism. It is here that the Gaelic Athletic Association has its headquarters.

National Museum of Ireland

One way of taking in a wide selection of knowledge of a country is by visiting its museums. The National Museum of Ireland includes modern exhibition galleries that showcase the rich culture and history of Ireland. And it is also surrounded by a beautiful lake and lush gardens.

When To Visit

Ireland's weather patterns can appear foreign to those who are not used to wet and windy weather. However, the rain tends to pour for about 150- 225 days. This does not mean that you will face wet weather throughout your traveling adventure. But it does mean that while you encounter wet weather during some mornings, the afternoon weather can be filled with brilliant sunshine. It is thus prudent to always be prepared. This way, you can enjoy indoor activities while it's soggy and outdoor activities while the weather is nice and warm. That being said, the warmest months are July and August while April, May and June present the sunniest months. However, apart from looking at the weather, you may want to visit Ireland during some festivals or events such as:

-Open House Dublin

Despite numerous places having a rich architectural background around the world, few of these places allow people to view such places for free. This is not the case in Dublin. Each year, over one hundred buildings in Dublin tend to open their doors to the public. This usually happens one weekend in October. During this weekend, you can explore to your heart's desire.

-Dublin Theatre Festival

For a rich cultural experience, watch out for the Dublin Theatre Festival (usually starting in late September), which usually runs for over two weeks. During this time, various titles are performed by different theatrical companies. The festival showcases both national and international theatre from select venues in Dublin. It comprises of tours, screenings, performances, and talks. It features the work of world-renowned playwrights and showcases Ireland in a way that is unforgettable.

Wexford Festival Opera

You can experience the 'buried operatic treasure' in Wexford (in late October). The Wexford Festival Opera is an event that has gained prominence on the Irish cultural calendar. It is simply a delight and has continued running for over sixty years. Its ability to revive and perform forgotten titles makes it a festival worth beholding.

How much it may cost

When planning how much to spend, you must take into account things like:

*Accommodation (and what the accommodation caters for)

*Transport (to and from different destinations)

*Tipping money (usually 10-15 percent of what you spend)

*Spending money (if you plan to purchase souvenirs or treat yourself to things not catered for under accommodation)

*Emergency cash (because sometimes accidents happen)

*Phone cash (because you may have to pay for your phone charges)

The important thing is to plan for the basics and ensure that you don't go beyond your budget. If you cannot afford to stay in a hotel (usually costing around €60 per night) , check out cheaper accommodation such as bed and breakfast (around €35), guest houses (around €45) or hostels. Compare the prices as these tend to differ and you can even find some more expensive than hotels.

Your stay in Ireland

Once you set up your trip to Ireland, there are some things you need to know in order to have a nice trip. Call it a survival guide.

-Passport or ID

Always carry your passport or ID even if you are not required to have one when you enter Ireland from your country of origin. You'll be far away from home and despite good intentions, anything can happen that will require you to identify yourself.

-Currency

You will have to use Euro notes when you are in the Irish Republic and the pound sterling (€) when you are in Northern Ireland. You can change your money at an ATM but ensure you inform your bank of your visit. This is because banks tend to stop transactions on your card if they see 'unusual' activity.

-Exchange rates

Exchange rates tend to vary from time to time but € is approximately $1.37 and 1 pound is approximately $1.66. Find out how much the rates go for before you plan on how to spend your cash. Instead of using a currency-exchange booth, go to an ATM or a bank to exchange your cash.

-Language

Many people in Ireland are well conversant with the English language. However, a small number of people speak Irish only. Signs and timetables tend to be written in both languages so you should have no difficulty navigating through the country.

-Safety

Although Ireland is a beautiful country worth exploring, there exist bad people in the world. Do not neglect your safety. Don't just leave your belongings all over or walk into dark alleys by yourself. And don't attempt to try out new ragged routes when you don't have a guide in the name of adventure. Keep vigilant even as you explore. It would be best to find out the phone number of the local tourist police just in case you encounter some trouble.

-Weather

The weather in Ireland changes – sometimes unexpectedly. You can find yourself experiencing all four seasons in one day. This means you need to always be prepared for the changing weather. Don't look out of the window and decide it's going to be warm especially if you plan to be gone the whole day. Pack your windbreaker and an umbrella just in case.

Environmental care

Don't damage the environment. Don't touch plants or feed animals because you admire them – you can end up harming them. Don't introduce anything new to the environment or take anything out of the environment. You found a beautiful place, leave it as it is and visit another day.

Conclusion

Traveling in Ireland is intended to be a unique, adventurous experience that will leave you with beautiful memories and a desire to come back another day. Plan your journey well and ensure you have the required documents, the cash you want to spend and the maps to where you plan to go. It would be best to book your accommodation before landing in Ireland especially during peak season. Endeavor to learn even as you undertake leisure activities and spend your time rejuvenating and relaxing.

Thank you again for downloading this book!

Finally, if you enjoyed this book, please share your thoughts and post a review on Amazon.

Thank you and good luck!

PS: Can I Ask You A Quick Favor?

If you liked the book, please leave a nice review on Amazon! I´d absolutely love to hear your feedback. Every time I read your reviews… you make me smile. I´d be immensely thankful if you go to Amazon now and write down a quick line sharing with me your experience. I personally read ALL the reviews there, and I´m thrilled to hear your feedback and honest motivation. It´s what keeps me going, and helps me improve everyday =)

<u>Please go Amazon Now and Drop A quick review sharing your experience !</u>

***

<u>THANKS!</u>

***

ONCE YOU´RE BACK,FLIP THE PAGE!

BONUS CHAPTER AHEAD

=)

Check Out My Other Books

Are you ready to exceed your limits? Then pick a book from the one below

If you´d like to see the entire list of all my books (there are a ton more!), go to :

http://www.amazon.com/s/ref=ntt_athr_dp_sr_1?_enco ding=UTF8&field-author=Allison%20Keys%20R&search-alias=digital-text&sort=relevancerank

Preview Of "Spain For Travelers"

Introduction

I want to thank you and congratulate you for downloading the book, *"Spanish: For Travelers! The Tourist Guide To Make The Most Out Of Your Trip To Spain – Discover Where To Go, Eat, Sleep & Party"*.

This book has all the information you need to make your trip to Spain memorable.

What comes to mind when you think of Spain? Depending on where you come from and your preferences, your thinking of Spain will be different. If you love football for instance, the mention of Messi, Xavi, Ronaldo, Rivaldo, Zidane, Maradona, Pele, Figo, Samuel Eto'o and Ronaldinho will probably make you remember La Liga. On the other hand, if you love mad partying, Ibiza would probably be the place you'd want to party before you die. Well, Spain has a lot more to offer than just that. For instance, it is home to 35 World Heritage Sites, home to the famous bull running and fighting (I know you've seen that in movies), and home to the world's famous tomato fighting festival where thousands of people fight with over 100 tons of ripe tomatoes. Besides, there is a lot more that the Spaniards have to offer than that.

Thanks again for downloading this book, I hope you enjoy it!

Spain (*España* in Spanish) is a sovereign state found in southwestern Europe on the Iberian Peninsula and is bordered by the Mediterranean Sea to the west. The capital city of Spain is Madrid, which is also the largest city, and the national language is Spanish.

Do you know that Spain has been rated first among the countries with the largest number of World Heritage Cities? It has also been rated second under the UNESCO World Heritage Sites, Italy coming first. This country is considered one of the most exotic countries in Europe due to its internationally recognized festivities and folklore, friendly inhabitants, the cuisine, relaxed lifestyle and the vibrant nightlife.

Spain: A Walk Down History Lane

Spain has undergone many changes through its unique history to become what it is now. The history up to now is one of the most fascinating in the world.

In the beginning

Migrations to Spain from Africa, The Mediterranean and Europe have been seen since the dawn of history. Phoenicians first came to Spain in the 6st century B.C and called it 'Span' which meant hidden land. The Romans conquered Spain by the dawn of the first century B.C, spreading Christianity. Later, the Visigoths (Germans from Europe) and Vandals brought down the Roman Empire to conquer Spain. Their rulers fought among themselves thus they were unstable. Muslims from Africa (known as the Moos in Spain's history) invaded Spain in the A.D 711 and conquered it. This led to the spread of Islamic culture across Spain. The Muslim rulers later introduced new irrigation systems and crops and increased trade in the country. They hit the peak of the tenth century as they also advanced medicine, mathematics, and philosophy leading to the Golden age of Islamic rule.

Christian kingdoms based in Northern Spain conquered the Muslims in 1492 and spread catholic religion. Spain acquired silver from the Americas thus enriching it. It became even more powerful during this period. Later, in the Napoleonic wars, Spain was taken over and the Christian kingdom lost power. This war ended in 1815.

During the 1930's, the Spanish civil war emerged, wiping out more than 500,000 people. Gen. Francisco Franco won and took over Spain as a brutal dictator until he died in 1975.

After Franco's death, the monarchy of Spain was restored. It began to change into an industrial, democratic, and modern European nation. During this time also, different political stripes were formed and the politicians suggested the division of Spain into 17 autonomous regions and succeeded. This became one of the most important times in the history of Spain since the country was transformed from one of the most centralized countries in the whole of Europe to the most decentralized. Spain has then after undergone many transformations.

Maps And Regions Of Spain

Spain is a state located in South Western Europe, which occupies 80% of the Iberian Peninsula (20% is occupied by Portugal). It borders the Mediterranean Sea and the North Atlantic Ocean, between France and Portugal. The country is 505,957 square kilometers in area and has a coastline of 4,964 km.

Spain is divided into seventeen autonomous/*autonomías* regions (communities) known as 'Comunidades Autónomas'. Each of these regions has its own unique features including historical traditions, government, and even official languages. The regions are further divided into 50 provinces ('provincias'). Below is an outline of the 17 regions:

Andalucía: This region is in the southern part of the Iberian Peninsula. They include: Almeria, Cádiz, Granada, Jaén, Sevilla, Malaga, Cordoba, and Huelva

Aragon: This region is in the northern. The capital of this region is Zaragoza. Provinces: Zaragoza, Teruel and Huesca.

Asturias: This region lies on the northern coast of Spain with Cantabria bordering it to the east and Galicia to the West. This region is a province also.

Balearic Islands (islas Baleares): This region is located near the eastern coast of Iberian Peninsula in the western

Mediterranean Sea. This region is also a province in its own.

Basque Country: This region is located on the Bay of Biscay and borders France. Provinces: Vizcaya, Álava and Guipúzcua.

Canary Islands: Located off the Northwest Coast of Africa. Provinces: Santa Cruz de Tenerife and Las Palmas.

Cantabria: This region is located at the Bay of Biscay on the lovely city of Santander. This region is a single province region.

Castilla La Mancha: This region lies between Andalucía and Madrid. Provinces: Guadalajara, Albacete, Cuenca, Toledo and Ciudad Real.

Castilla y Léon: This region is the largest of all the autonomous regions of Spain and borders Portugal and ten of the other regions. Provinces: Valladolid, Léon, Burgos, Segovia, Soria, Zamora, Salamanca, Palencia, Avila.

Catalonia: The capital of this region is the world famous Barcelona. Catalonia is located in the northeast of Spain. Provinces: Barcelona, Lleida, Girona and Tarragona.

Extremadura: This region is in the west of Spain and borders Portugal. Provinces: Badajoz and Caceres.

Galicia: Galicia is at the very northwest area of Spain. Its capital is A Coruña. Provinces: A Coruña, Lugo, Pontevedra and Orense.

La Rioja: La Rioja is located Northern Spain and is a single province region.

Madrid: This region is the capital of Spain and is located in central Spain. It is one of the most autonomous regions of the country. This region is also a province on its own.

Murcia: Murcia is located in the eastern areas of Spain. This region has no provinces.

Navarra: Located on Northern Spain.

Valencia: This region stretches along the Mediterranean coast from Murcia to Catalonia. Provinces: Valencia, Alicante and Castellon.

To help you understand this better, here is a map showing the 17 regions.

Where To Stay In Spain

Spain offers a wide variety of accommodation for you to choose from ranging from hostels, hotels, resorts, rented villas, home stays, and small tourist friendly villages to camping and also monasteries. The prices of all these accommodation facilities vary so as to suite your budget. Below are some good places you can find accommodation. We will talk about the accommodation options:

Note: Ensure you don't get tricked by mid-range hotels and some guest houses with the '10% VAT is not included' trick. These hidden charges are often put in small print, which can be ignored if you are not careful. In Spanish, VAT is IVA.

Small villages: These tourist friendly villages (such as Alquezar) can be a good place to live in if you are traveling on budget.

Casa rural: This is the B&B of Spain. Although the name suggests the location being rural, this is not necessarily true. You will find these in virtually every province hence making them a great place to reside in if you are traveling on budget. They are also highly controlled and inspected although the prices and quality vary.

Hotels: Spain has many luxury, budget and mid range hotels that you can choose. You can be sure that you won't be short of options irrespective of your budget.

Paradores: These are state owned 3-5 star hotels founded in 1928 in the rein of the Spanish King Alfonso XIII. They are often located in different historical buildings like Moorish castles (such as Alhambra), convents, or haciendas. When you stay in these, you can be sure that you will have easy access to some of the famous historic places. Places with these include Santiago de Campostela, Ronda, Arcos de la Frontera and Santillana del Mar among other places spread all over Spain (over 100). Rates here go for about €85 for a double room to €245 for twin room. Breakfast in many of these is served for about €10.

Hostels: Spain has many hostels spread all over the country with rates varying between €15 and €25 per night.

Apartment rental: If you are looking for short term (over one week) self catering option, you can check these out.

Camping: This is the most affordable way to get accommodation in Spain.

Here are some few hotels and hostels to check out.

Hotels

Hotel Mar I Vent

This hotel is located in Banyalbufar, Balearic Islands. Contact: +34 971 61 80 00, the price for this hotel ranges from 98 – 150 Euros per night.

Finca Santa Marta

It is located in Trujillo, Extremadura. The prices per night range from 60 – 85 Euros per night. For reservation, you can contact the hotel at Tel: +34 927 31 92 03, Mobile: +34 658 91 43 55, email: henri@faclinet.es

Posada De San Jose

This hotel is located in Cuenca, Castilla-La Mancha and costs approximately 42-162 Euros per night. Contact Tel: +34 969 21 13 00 for reservations.

Hotel Posada Del Valle

It is located in Collia, Asturias with its price per night, ranging from 64 to 89 Euros per night. For any inquiries or booking, contact +34 985 84 11 57.

Hotel AC Palacio Del Carmen

This hotel is located in Santiago de Compostela, Galicia. The price for this hotel per night is from 80-200 Euros depending on the room and time of the year. You can contact +34 981 55 24 44 for bookings.

Hotel Aigua Blava

It is located in Aiguablava, Cataluña and will cost you approximately 175 – 265 Euros for each night. Contact; +34 972 62 20 58

Hotel Albucasis

This one is located at Córdoba, Andalucía. The hotel charges approximately 50-85 Euros per night. Contact: +34 957 47 86 25.

Hotel Asturias

It is located at Calle Sevilla in Madrid City Centre. Tel+34 914 29 66 76,

http://www.hotel-asturias.com

Hostels

Hostel One Paralelo

This hostel is located in Barcelona and charges approximately 12 Euros per night per person. Contact; +34 934 43 98 85

Sant Jordi Hostel Rock Palace

Located in carrer Balmes, Barcelona and costs each person roughly 11 Euros per night. Contact: +34 934 533 281

Sungate Hostel

This hostel is located in Madrid and charges approximately 17 Euros for each person per night. Contact: +34 910 23 68 06

Way Hostel

Located in Calle Relatores, Madrid and costs about 13 Euros for one person per night. For bookings and reservations, contact: +34 914 20 05 83.

La Banda Rooftop Hostel

This hostel is located in Calle Dos Mayo, Sevilla and charges roughly 20 Euros per night per person. Contact: +34 955 22 81 18.

Toc Hostel Sevilla

It is located in Calle Miguel Manara, Sevilla. This hostel charges about 17 Euros for a night per head. Contact: +34 954 50 12 44

Samay Hostel Sevilla

This hostel is located in Av. De Menendez Pelayo, Sevilla. You can contact +34 955 10 01 60 for reservations and bookings. It charges about 19 Euros per person.

Hostal Antares

This hostel is situated in Calle Cetti Meriem, Granada. This hostel charges 12 Euros per person per night. Contact: +34 958 22 83 13

White Nest Hostel

This hostel is located at Calle Santisimo San Pedro, Granada. For reservation or inquiries, contact +34 958 99 47 14. This hostel will cost you approximately 15 Euros per night.

43402189R00034

Made in the USA
Lexington, KY
28 July 2015